Mel B.

Step 11

Partnership With A High Power

Revised Edition

Hazelden Publishing
Center City, Minnesota 55012-0176

ISBN: 978-0-89486-0160-4

Editor's note

The Twelve Steps are reprinted with permission of
Alcoholics Anonymous World Services, Inc. Permission to reprint the Twelve Steps does not mean that
Alcoholics Anonymous has reviewed or approved the
contents of this publication, nor that AA agrees with
the views expressed herein. The views expressed
herein are solely those of the author. AA is a program of recovery from alcoholism. Use of the Twelve
Steps in connection with programs and activities that
are patterned after AA, but that address other problems, does not imply otherwise.

Sought through prayer and meditation to improve our conscious contact with God as we understood Him, praying only for knowledge of His will for us and the power to carry that out.

—STEP ELEVEN

Partnership with a Higher Power

Before finding sobriety in Alcoholics Anonymous, I displayed great faith and remarkable persistence--in drinking. I worshiped the bottle; I took every problem to the bottle; I leaned on the bottle with almost childlike trust. I persisted in this sick devotion long after the bottle had repeatedly betrayed me and wrecked my life.

After finding AA, I still needed faith and persistence—but with a new direction and a new focus. I looked to a Higher Power for the answers I had vainly sought in the bottle. This quest took faith, it took persistence, and it took a strong determination to succeed in sobriety. But the Higher Power I found in AA has been a reliable guide and partner, never once betraying me. It's repairing the wreckage of my past and providing a new way of life. Through the guidance of the Twelve Step program, I've been able to maintain and thoroughly enjoy my new way of life.

It's not always easy to maintain this new way of life. Nearly every recovering alcoholic and addict faces the boredom and disillusionment that may set in after the early glow of inspiration and excitement has faded. But the Twelve Step program of recovery is structured to help us face these dangers. Step Eleven reminds us that we need to hold on to the wonderful way of life we've been given.

Step Eleven is no quick fix. It is really Steps Two and Three practiced on a *daily* basis. Step Eleven can be our guide for the rest of our lives. If Step Eleven is properly understood and carefully followed, some of the changes in our lives will border on the miraculous. We can have continuous sobriety, along with growth in the qualities we sought in our drug of choice but never found.

Step Eleven does exact a price, however, and we must pay it if we expect favorable results. There is a price in giving up the self-will that led us into trouble. Part of the price is working to become open-minded and willing about our need to change. Finally, Step Eleven calls for faith and persistence— the very qualities that we applied so wrongly to our drinking or drug using!

The plan and purpose

We started to pick up the basics of Step Eleven when we worked Steps Two and Three. These basics, which we learn from AA and other recovery literature and from others' experience, tell us that we can find a Higher Power who will be a personal source of both *guidance* and *power*. This Higher Power can be God or whatever else we choose to believe it to be. The program doesn't directly tell us what to believe about the nature of our Higher Power. It does imply that our Higher Power is loving and has only our best interests at heart. A definition of Higher Power is even suggested in the Second Tradition of AA:

"A loving God as He may express Himself in our group conscience."*

The program also includes the idea that this loving power wants to enrich our lives. All of us wanted the abundant life and deluded ourselves into thinking that alcohol and other drugs would give that blessed state to us. How exciting to realize that we truly can have an abundant life if we accept the protection and care of our Higher Power. The AA pioneers, even when they were a small group of about 100 recovering alcoholics, believed that such a life could be had for the asking. "We found that God does not make too hard terms with those who seek Him," they wrote. "To us, the Realm of Spirit is broad, roomy, all inclusive; never exclusive or forbidding to those who earnestly seek."**

Step Eleven provides a search *plan* for those who wish to enter this Realm of Spirit. The search for a Higher Power takes place in our own thinking. "Sought through prayer and meditation" deals solely with our personal ways of communicating with our Higher Power. This is an individual matter, and what works best for one person might be irritating to another. What counts is not the style or manner of our prayer but the effects produced in our lives.

Early AA members in Akron and New York had group prayer on their knees, a practice abandoned by the Twelve Step fellowship in the early 1940s. It isn't necessary that we pray on our knees, unless as individuals we feel it makes our prayer more effective.

Twelve Steps and Twelve Traditions (New York: AA World Services, Inc., 1989), 132.
** *Alcoholics Anonymous* [The Big Book], 3d ed. (New York: AA World Services, Inc., 1976), 46.

Nor is it necessary to pray in the company of others, unless that is our preference.

Purpose also is included in Step Eleven. The purpose of prayer and meditation is to improve one's *conscious contact* with the God of our understanding. How can we tell if we're getting anywhere with our prayers and meditations? There should be signs along the way to tell us if we're on the right path. One sign is a deep sense of gratitude, accompanied by a feeling of belonging in the world. We should experience growth in self-esteem and perhaps a feeling that we have rights and an understanding that we are worthy. We may have a sense of being guided and cared for as we go about our affairs. We may even experience an occasional sense of joy about sobriety and work.

The mystery of guidance

There are, however, dangers and difficulties in the prayer and meditation program. Our minds are like early radio receiving sets, which picked up static and conflicting messages. We ought to seek guidance, and we are often told to do so by our sponsors and other people in the program. Yet, seeking guidance can be a very tricky matter and for very understandable reasons.

Bill W., the AA co-founder who wrote most of the AA program materials, issued a warning to the person who tries to run his or her life rigidly or make self-serving demands upon God. In *Twelve Steps and Twelve Traditions,* Bill wrote about such a person: "To any questioning or criticism of his actions he instantly proffers his reliance upon prayer for guidance in all matters great or small. He may have forgotten the possibility that his own wishful thinking and the human tendency to rationalize have distorted his so-called guidance. With the best of intentions, he tends to force his own will into all sorts of situations and problems with the comfortable assurance that he is acting under God's specific direction. Under such an illusion, he can of course create great havoc without in the least intending it."*

In Step Eleven, guidance also is defined as "knowledge of God's will for us and the power to carry that out." This means that we do not seek guidance *for* others, but try to learn how we can be of service *to* others.

But how are we to know the will of our Higher Power? Here again, the messages can be difficult to understand, like the stuff coming over that early receiving set. Our own desires and opinions are so much a part of us that we are likely to view the will of a Higher Power in terms of our own feelings. Superstition and early religious training can play a part in this. Years ago, one of my friends suffered greatly because he did not believe God would ever forgive him for his years of drinking. This belief was harmful, because he did not think he could please God or was worthy of God's help. I have known others who believe that God wants them to suffer or to fail in something, and these beliefs tend to become self-fulfilling.

When my confusion on this subject becomes too thick, I've found comfort in the ancient parable of the Prodigal Son, which seems almost custom-made for the recovering alcoholic or addict. In this parable,

---

Twelve Steps and Twelve Traditions, 103-104.

the father, who represents God, runs to meet the son even though he has wasted his inheritance in selfish, sinful behavior. The son is so beaten that he has decided not to ask his father for anything, and yet the father gives him a ring, beautiful clothing, and holds a celebration because the son has returned!

But there also is an Elder Brother in this parable, a person who always did his duty and never left his father. He is extremely displeased about the favorable treatment of his younger brother and refuses to take part in the celebration.

The lesson? God seeks us even more than we seek him. There are, however, two parts of our nature that are in conflict: We are both the Younger Brother and the Elder Brother. God wants to give us everything and wants complete union with us, for no other reason than that we are God's children. But there is a stern Elder Brother within us who holds back and tells us we must earn everything, that only righteous and deserving people are entitled to union with God.

The Younger Brother side of our nature (the rebellious, self-centered side) also must make a concession in order to make contact with a Higher Power. This concession is the complete willingness to accept God's will on whatever terms are offered. In the parable, for example, the Prodigal Son was so defeated he was even willing to be a servant in his father's house. Although his father surprised him with love and gifts, none of these benefits were obtained by *demanding* them or by pleading and begging. Many of us who come to a recovery program have the same experience. We're no longer in a position to demand anything, and the best we can hope for is relief from the terrible agony of our alcoholism or drug addiction. We are, therefore, often surprised by unexpected improvements in other areas of our lives.

Step Eleven keeps this idea before us: We don't *demand* anything from our Higher Power. The *best* method for meeting our needs will always occur if we leave matters to God. This, of course, is not the way we like to work. We are tempted to give orders, to pray things like "I want *this* job!" or "I want *this* person to marry me!" or "I want *this* problem cleared up in *this* manner by next Tuesday!"

In fact, we don't have to tell our Higher Power what we need or what will be best for us. The Greek philosopher Pythagoras expressed a similar thought, "Do not pray for yourself: You do not know what will help you." This simply means that we cannot see the Big Picture, only a part of it. We often can't perceive the long-term effects of something that seems attractive and reasonable at the moment. But if we pray and meditate in the right way, some of these things will be made clear to us.

One AA member, for example, became quite disappointed when he prayed for guidance about a business negotiation, which later fell through. Had he succeeded, he would have missed an even better opportunity a few weeks later.

In 1935, Bill W. suffered a harsh setback when he was defeated in a proxy fight for control of a small machine tool company. His desperation drove him to get in touch with another alcoholic, Dr. Bob, who joined him in founding AA.

We never really know when defeats will become victories. There is a saying, frequently heard in AA, that warns us to be careful what we pray for, because we might get it! The point is that what we want today could be exactly what we don't want six months from now.

A harmony of wills

What we want is not always wrong, and just because it's our will doesn't necessarily mean it's against the will of our Higher Power. As recovering people, our common failure is not that our aims are wrong; it lies in not seeking the *highest* and *best* that is possible for us.

It is also true that God's will for us must be related to our natural talents and abilities and the circumstances of our lives. We can take ourselves as we are at this point and seek to merge our own aims and purposes with God's plan.

As recovering alcoholics and addicts, we can make some reasonable assumptions about God's will in our lives. One, God wants us to stay sober and to help others. We feel this strongly at many Twelve Step meetings or when we reflect on what has happened in our lives. We can look upon our Twelve Step fellowship as a channel of God's grace. Although certainly not the only channel, it is probably the best one for recovering people.

God's will means carrying out our reasonable duties and meeting our responsibilities. Alcohol and other drugs cause us to neglect our families and to ignore other responsibilities. A solid spiritual program built on Step Eleven will give us the maturity and strength to do the right things for ourselves, for our families, in our jobs, and toward society.

As recovering people we each have a part to play in life. Each of us has things that only we can do and a place that only we can fill. Some of the good work we could do—particularly in our Twelve Step fellowship—might never be done unless we do it.

Whatever we learn about our Higher Power's will for us, we shouldn't forget that we have been given the power to carry it out—Step Eleven implicitly states that. In some ways it may be similar to carrying out an assignment from an employer. If the company expects you to make a business trip, it will usually provide expense money, credit cards, introductions, and other necessities. God seems to work in the same way. For example, the early AA members, even in the depth of the Depression, always got by and always had the funds to carry out their work.

We have work to do for a higher employer who wants to provide for us. This is important work, and it requires a merging of our wills and God's will. Like the father of the Prodigal Son, God needs us just as much as we need God. But we also have to accept God's *plan* and *purpose*. Without conscious contact with a Higher Power, we can't do the things we really need to do.

The Twelve Steps of Alcoholics Anonymous[*]

1. We admitted we were powerless over alcohol—that our lives had become unmanageable.
2. Came to believe that a Power greater than ourselves could restore us to sanity.
3. Made a decision to turn our will and our lives over to the care of God *as we understood Him.*
4. Made a searching and fearless moral inventory of ourselves.
5. Admitted to God, to ourselves, and to another human being the exact nature of our wrongs.
6. Were entirely ready to have God remove all these defects of character.
7. Humbly asked Him to remove our shortcomings.
8. Made a list of all persons we had harmed, and became willing to make amends to them all.
9. Made direct amends to such people wherever possible, except when to do so would injure them or others.
10. Continued to take personal inventory and when we were wrong promptly admitted it.
11. Sought through prayer and meditation to improve our conscious contact with God *as we understood Him,* praying only for knowledge of His will for us and the power to carry that out.
12. Having had a spiritual awakening as the result of these steps, we tried to carry this message to alcoholics, and to practice these principles in all our affairs.

---

[*]The Twelve Steps of AA are taken from *Alcoholics Anonymous,* 3d ed., published by AA World Services, Inc., New York, N.Y., 59-60. Reprinted with permission of AA World Services, Inc. (See editor's note on the copyright page.)